Every Which Way for Ramen!

A Ramen Lovers Cookbook: 50 Ways to Enjoy Ramen

BY

Daniel Humphreys

Copyright 2019 Daniel Humphreys

License Notes

No part of this Book can be reproduced in any form or by any means including print, electronic, scanning or photocopying unless prior permission is granted by the author.

All ideas, suggestions and guidelines mentioned here are written for informative purposes. While the author has taken every possible step to ensure accuracy, all readers are advised to follow information at their own risk. The author cannot be held responsible for personal and/or commercial damages in case of misinterpreting and misunderstanding any part of this Book

Table of Contents

Introduction 6

    Pineapple Salsa Ramen 7

    Steak and Rice Ramen 9

    Cajun Shrimp & Ramen 11

    Chicken, Corn, & Tofu Ramen 13

    Andouille Ramen 15

    BLT Ramen Bowl 17

    BLT & Avocado Ramen Bowl 19

    Ramen Italian Chowder 21

    Cucumber and Zucchini Ramen 24

    Okra & Ramen Medley 27

    Cheesy Ham and Ramen 29

    Refried Enchiladas 31

    Poormans Steak and Broccoli 33

    Artic Ranch & Prosciutto Ramen 35

    Cannellini Soup 37

Ramen Spaghetti with Mini Meatballs 39

Ramen Chicken Pot Pie 41

Mojo Chicken Ramen 43

Black Bean and Tomato Ramen 45

Ramen Broccoli Soup 47

Cheesy Ramen Soup 49

Ham and Ramen Stew 51

Air Fryer Chicken Sandwich and Basil-Ramen 53

Thyme Ramen 55

Apple- Chicken Sausage and Ramen 57

Spicy Shrimp Ramen 59

Crab & Ramen 61

Shrimp & Smoky Ramen 63

Pimento and Ramen 65

Chipotle Chicken Ramen 67

Coconut Shrimp & Ramen 69

Prosciutto & Ramen 71

Ramen Aus Jus 73

Bacon Cheeseburger Ramen 75

Ramen, Bean and Bacon Soup 77

Bleu Ramen 79

Siracha Ranch Ramen 81

Pepperoni Pizza with Ramen 83

Chicken Sausage in a Red Pepper and Ginger Broth 85

Cucumber, Zucchini & Ramen Pasta 87

Spiraled Tuna Pasta 89

Chili Ramen 91

Red Pepper & Jalapeno Ramen 93

Ramen Italiano 95

Greek & Ramen Pasta 97

Tex-Mex Ramen 99

Pulled Pork Burrito 101

Red Pepper & Corn Pasta 103

Cajun Ramen 105

Author's Afterthoughts 107

About the Author 108

5

Introduction

Tired of the same old ramen dishes? With this excellent cookbook recipes are specifically design to bring out the big bold flavors you desire of ramen. Excellent flavor pairings to create the dishes you crave without hard to find, expensive ingredients. Eating well doesn't have to break the bank or be the equivalent of a scavenger hunt.

Pineapple Salsa Ramen

Why eat ordinary ramen? Makes 2 servings

Ingredients:

- 1 package ramen noodles (w/o seasoning)
- ½-pound ground beef
- 1/2 packet no sodium taco seasoning (such as Mrs. Dash)
- 1 tablespoons low sodium pineapple salsa
- 1 can washed low-sodium black beans
- 1 cup worth julienned onions and bell peppers-or-diced jalapenos
- 5-6 cups low sodium beef broth

Directions:

In medium size pot or skillet with high sides, brown ground beef, stir in seasoning; drain on paper towels for 5 minutes and return to pot or skillet; stir in beans, salsa, onions, peppers, broth, ramen; bring to a boil, reduce heat, cover, let simmer 8-9 minutes

Steak and Rice Ramen

Let the meat come to room temperature before cooking!

Makes 2 servings

Ingredients:

- ¾ tablespoon olive oil
- 1 cup of diced steak
- 1 1/3cups leftover rice
- ½ tsp Italian seasoning
- 1 can no salt added crushed tomatoes
- 1 package ramen noodles (w/o seasoning)
- 5-6 cups low sodium beef or vegetable broth

Directions:

In warm pot or skillet with high sides, on medium high heat brown steak, stir in rice, Italian seasoning, ramen, broth; bring to a boil, reduce heat, cover, let simmer 8-9 minutes

Cajun Shrimp & Ramen

Works with crawfish too! Makes 2 servings

Ingredients:

- 1 tablespoon olive oil
- 1-2 cups salad shrimp
- 1 packet – low, or, no salt- Cajun seasoning
- 1 onion diced
- 1 bell pepper diced -or- 1 diced jalapeno
- 1 tomato diced
- 1 avocado diced
- ½ cup chopped spinach
- 1 can low sodium black beans washed and drained
- 1 cup shredded Monterey jack cheese
- 1 package ramen noodles (w/o seasoning)
- 5-6 cups beef broth

Directions:

In a pot or skillet with high sides bring to heat over a burner set for med-high heat; add oil, shrimp, onion, pepper, and seasoning; sauté 1 minute; add in tomatoes, avocado, beans, cheese, noodles, broth; bring to a boil, reduce heat, cover, let simmer 8-9 minutes

Chicken, Corn, & Tofu Ramen

Also, makes a great vegetarian meal! Makes 2 servings

Ingredients:

- 2 cups diced pre-cooked chicken
- 1 cup whole kernel corn
- 2/3-¾ cup diced roasted red pepper
- 1 block silken cubed tofu
- ½ Tbsp. chopped parsley
- ½ tsp minced garlic
- 2-3 large basil leaves sliced
- 1 egg
- 1 package ramen noodles (w/o seasoning)
- 5-6 cups low sodium chicken broth

Directions:

Bring pot or high side skillet to heat; add in chicken broth let come to a boil; stir in egg ½ tsp at a time; stir in parsley, garlic, basil, tofu, roasted red pepper, corn, chicken pieces; bring to a boil, reduce heat, cover, let simmer 8-9 minutes

Andouille Ramen

Also, great with chicken-apple sausage! Makes 2 servings

Ingredients:

- 1 Tbsp olive oil
- 1 link andouille sausage diced
- 1 cup spinach chopped
- 1 can no-salt added petite diced tomatoes
- 1 can no-salt added diced sweet potatoes
- ½ cup diced black olives
- ½ cup red roasted peppers
- Juice of ½ lime
- ½ tablespoon chili powder
- 2 teaspoon cumin
- 1/3 cup salsa
- 2 cups shredded Monterey jack cheese
- 1 package ramen noodles
- 5-6 cups low-sodium beef or vegetable broth

Directions:

In a pot or high walled skillet mix together oil, chili powder, cumin, sausage slices; sauté 1-2 minutes; add in spinach, tomatoes, sweet potatoes, olives, roasted peppers; mix together and stir 45 seconds to 1 minute; stir in salsa, lime juice, cheese, ramen, and broth; bring to a boil, reduce heat, cover, let simmer 8-9 minutes

BLT Ramen Bowl

For extra crunch, add walnuts or pinenuts! Makes 2 servings

Ingredients:

- 1 cup ramen noodles cooked as directed
- 1 cup diced turkey bacon
- 1 cup petite diced tomato
- 1 cup shredded lettuce
- 2 tablespoons mango salsa
- 5-10 cubes of various cheeses

Directions:

On plate lay out noodles; place on top, or on the side: bacon, tomato, lettuce, cheese

BLT & Avocado Ramen Bowl

Great for a light lunch! Makes 2 serving

Ingredients:

- 1 package ramen noodles cooked as directed
- 1 cup diced turkey bacon
- 1 cup diced tomato
- 1 cup shredded lettuce
- 1 avocado diced
- 2 tablespoons mango salsa
- 5-10 cubes of various cheese

Directions:

On a plate lay out noodles; put on top, or on the side: bacon, tomato, lettuce, avocado, salsa, cheese

Ramen Italian Chowder

Try it with Greek Seasoning! Makes 2 servings

Ingredients:

- 1 Tbsp canola oil
- 1 minced onion
- 1 tsp minced garlic
- 1 cup ground beef
- 1 cup diced bacon
- 1 cup no-salt added crushed tomato
- 1 cup chopped kale
- ½ whole kernel corn
- 2 cups chopped bok choy or celery
- 1 tsp Italian seasoning
- 1 cup shredded cheddar cheese
- 2 Tbsp diced parsley divided
- 1 package ramen
- 5-6 cups low-sodium beef broth

Directions:

In pot or high walled skillet pour in oil, onion, and garlic; sauté 1 minute; stir in ground beef and turkey bacon; browned ground beef and drain 5 minutes; wipe out pot or skillet and return ground beef and turkey mixture; return to med-high heat and mix together tomato, kale, corn, bok choy or celery, ramen, broth; bring to a boil, reduce heat, cover, let simmer 8-9 minutes; fix two bowls and top each with cheese and parsley

Cucumber and Zucchini Ramen

For extra health benefits add turmeric and lima beans!
Makes 2 servings

24

Ingredients:

- 1 Tablespoon butter
- 1 diced shallot
- ½ Tablespoon brown sugar
- ½ teaspoon Worchester sauce
- 1 can no-salt added sliced new potatoes
- 1 tsp smoked paprika
- 1 cup cucumber spirals
- 1 cup zucchini spirals
- 1 cup macadamia nuts
- 1 package ramen
- 5-6 cups low sodium chicken broth
- 1 cup shredded Monterey jack cheese divided
- 1 teaspoon chives chopped divided
- 1 teaspoon Italian oregano chopped divided

Directions:

In pot or high walled skillet over med-high heat melt butter, stir in onions, brown sugar, Worchester sauce; sauté onions 4-5 minutes; stir in potatoes; sprinkle with paprika; cook 1-2 minutes; stir in cucumber spirals, zucchini spirals, macadamia nuts, ramen, broth; bring to a boil, reduce heat, cover, let simmer 8-9 minutes; ladle into two bowls; top with cheese, oregano, and chives

Okra & Ramen Medley

Try them with Great Northern Beans or Black-Eyed Peas!

Makes 2 servings

Ingredients:

- 1 cup baby spinach leaves
- 2 Roma tomatoes diced
- 1 onion diced
- 1 teaspoon minced garlic
- Juice of 1 lime
- 1 cup whole kernel corn
- 1 teaspoons smoked paprika
- ¾ cup okra
- 1 cup pinto beans (pre-cooked)
- ½ tablespoon diced cilantro
- 1/2 teaspoon chopped thyme
- 1 package ramen
- 5-6 cup of water

Directions:

In pot or high walled skillet mix together baby spinach leaves, tomatoes, onion, garlic, lime juice, corn, paprika, okra, pinto beans, cilantro, thyme, ramen, water; bring to boil, reduce heat, cover, let simmer 8-9 minutes

Cheesy Ham and Ramen

Try it with pepper jack cheese! Makes 2 servings

Ingredients:

- 1 package ramen
- 1 cup diced ham
- 1 cup broccoli pieces
- ¾ cup tri-pepper mix (diced red, yellow, green bell pepper mix)
- 3-4 basil leaves sliced
- ½ teaspoon parsley diced
- 1/2 teaspoon celery salt or seed
- 1 cup shredded cheddar cheese
- 3 cups low sodium chicken broth

Directions:

In pot or high walled skillet mix together ramen, ham, broccoli, peppers, basil, parsley, celery salt/seed, cheese, broth; bring to a boil, reduce heat, cover, let simmer 8-9 minutes

Refried Enchiladas

Also great with ground beef and taco seasoning! Makes 2 servings

Ingredients:

- 1 package ramen cooked as directed
- 1 Tbsp olive oil
- 2 cups shredded chicken
- 1 shallot diced
- 1 tsp minced garlic
- 1 small can tomato sauce
- 1 teaspoon chili powder
- 1/2 teaspoon cumin
- 1 can low sodium refried beans
- 1 cup shredded mozzarella cheese or queso melting cheese

Directions:

In a pot or high walled skillet over med-high heat, add oil, chicken, onion, garlic; sauté 2 minutes; pour in tomato sauce, chili powder, cumin, refried beans; on plate make a bed of ramen and ladle Refried Enchiladas on top; top with cheese

Poormans Steak and Broccoli

Also, great with seasonal fruits and veggies! Makes 2 servings

Ingredients:

- 1 julienned sweet onion
- 2 thinly sliced cloves of garlic
- 2 cups thinly sliced steak
- 1 cup thinly diced bok choy
- 1 cup soy beans
- ¼ cup diced parsley
- ½ tablespoon low sodium soy sauce
- ½ teaspoon sesame oil
- ½ teaspoon pepper
- ½ teaspoon red pepper flakes
- 1 package ramen
- 3 cups beef broth

Directions:

In high walled skillet sauté onion and garlic 2-3 minutes; steak, bok choy, soy beans, parsley, soy sauce, sesame oil, pepper, red pepper flakes, ramen, broth; bring to a boil, reduce heat, cover, let simmer 8-9 minutes

Artic Ranch & Prosciutto Ramen

Serve with crunchy bread and good wine! Makes 2 servings

Ingredients:

- 1 cup diced prosciutto
- 1 diced onion
- 1 diced green bell pepper
- 1 8 oz. can no salt added tomato sauce
- 1 packet ranch seasoning
- 1 package ramen
- 5 cups low sodium chicken broth
- 1 Tbsp diced cilantro (optional)
- 2 cups shredded Monterey jack cheese or habanero cheddar

Directions:

In a pot or high walled skillet warmed over med-high heat, combine: prosciutto, onion, bell pepper, tomatoes, ranch seasoning, ramen, broth, cilantro; bring to a boil, reduce heat, cover, let simmer 8-9 minutes; put ramen into two bowls, top each with cheese

Cannellini Soup

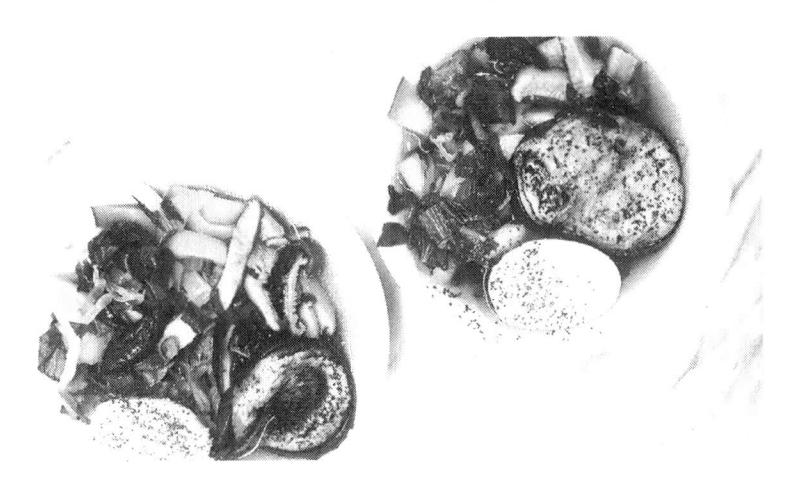

For extra texture add sweet potatoes and black olives!

Makes 2 servings

Ingredients:

- 1 can washed cannellini beans
- 1 cup diced eggplant
- 1 diced avocado
- 3 diced scallions
- 1 cup chopped seaweed
- 1 teaspoon jalapeno powder
- 1 package ramen
- 5 cups low sodium beef, vegetable, or ham broth
- 1 cup Italian blend shredded cheese or Monterey jack cheese

Directions:

In a pot combine: beans, eggplant, avocado, scallions, seaweed, jalapeno powder, ramen, broth; ladle into two serving bowls and top with cheese

Ramen Spaghetti with Mini Meatballs

Sliced hot dogs are also a great addition! Makes 2 servings

Ingredients:

- ½ lbs. ground beef
- 1 egg
- ½ cup breadcrumbs
- 1 Tbsp olive oil
- 1 package ramen
- ½ Tbsp. Italian seasoning
- 8 oz. tomato sauce
- 1 tablespoon dry white wine
- 3-4 cups low sodium beef broth
- 1 cups shredded cheddar cheese
- 1 cup shredded mozzarella or sharp white cheddar

Directions:

In a bowl mix together ground beef, egg, breadcrumbs; mix together with your hands and form into mini meatballs; pour olive oil over skillet on high; once hot add meatballs; let sit for thirty seconds and turn (tongs work best for this) and let cook 30 seconds; add in around the meatballs uncooked ramen; meanwhile, in a separate bowl mix together sauce, wine, broth and Italian seasoning; pour on top of ramen; top liberally with cheese; let simmer 8-10 minutes

Ramen Chicken Pot Pie

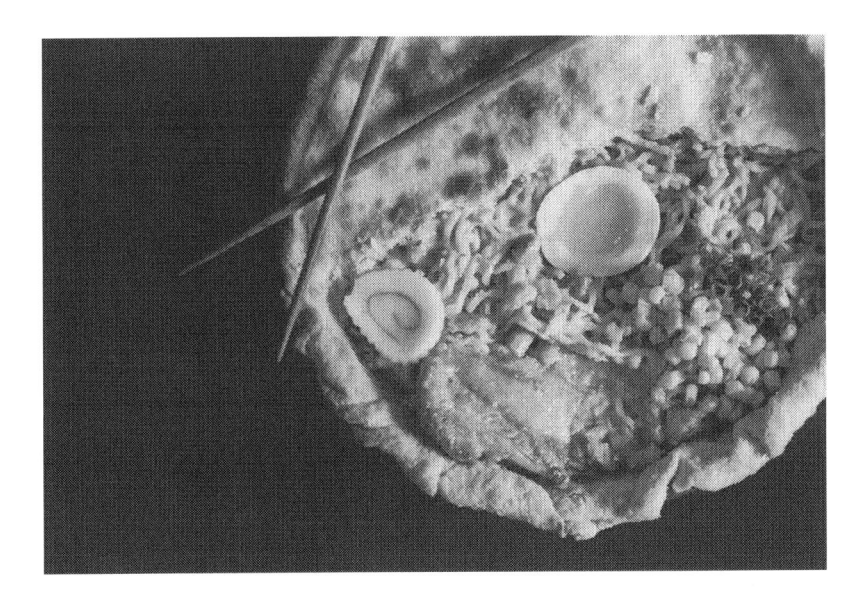

Serve with crunchy Italian bread! Makes 2 servings

Ingredients:

- 2 cups shredded chicken
- 1 can low sodium condensed cream of chicken soup
- 1 tsp Italian seasoning
- 1 can low sodium veggie mix
- 1 package ramen cooked as directed
- ½ cup low sodium chicken broth
- Shredded mozzarella and provolone cheese

Directions:

In skillet combine: chicken, condensed soup, seasoning, veggie mix, ramen, broth, cheese; stir well, let simmer 5-10 minutes, serve

Mojo Chicken Ramen

If you like Bahama Breeze's chicken, you'll like this!
Makes 2 servings

Ingredients:

- 1 package ramen
- ½ diced onion
- 1 teaspoon minced garlic
- 3 chopped jalapenos or bell peppers
- 1 cup shredded or diced chicken
- 2 cups low sodium mojo liquid marinade
- ½ teaspoon pepper

Directions:

In skillet sweat onion, garlic, jalapeno over low heat 10-15 minutes; add in chicken, 1/3 cup worth of marinade and pepper; toss in ramen; warm through

Black Bean and Tomato Ramen

Best when served at room temperature or medium heat!

Makes 2 servings

Ingredients:

- 1 package ramen cooked as directed
- 1 can low sodium black beans, wash and dry
- 1 cup diced fresh tomatoes
- 3 sliced large basil leaves
- 1 Tbsp diced parsley
- ½ tsp red pepper flakes
- 1/3 cup extra virgin olive oil
- ¼ tsp red wine vinegar or rice vinegar

Directions:

In a small air tight container mix together olive oil, vinegar, red pepper flakes, parsley, basil; cover and store in refrigerator; Mix together cooked ramen, beans, tomatoes; top with dressing and toss

Ramen Broccoli Soup

Ramen comfort food! Makes 2 servings

Ingredients:

- 1/4 cup butter
- 1/4 cup chopped shallot
- 1/4 cup all-purpose flour or equivalent thicking agent
- ½ can condensed cream of broccoli soup
- 1 can Almond Evaporated Milk
- 1/2 cup chicken broth
- ½ cup water
- 1 package ramen

Directions:

In a pot or high-walled skillet, add butter and shallot; sauté 1-2 minutes; stir in flour; stir in condensed soup, milk, chicken broth, water; stir well and let simmer 5 minutes; stir in noodles; cover and let simmer 5 more minutes

Cheesy Ramen Soup

Great for Halloween or fall; Makes 2 servings

Ingredients:

- 1 can cheese sauce -or- 3 cups shredded cheddar cheese
- 1 can low sodium blackbeans washed and drained
- 1 can no-salt added corn
- 3-4 cups okra
- 4 cups low sodium chicken broth or beef broth
- 2/3 cup water
- 1 tablespoon diced cilantro
- 1 tablespoon diced parsley

Directions:

In large pot melt cheese; stir in chicken broth and water; stir in black beans, corn, okra, cilantro, parsley

Ham and Ramen Stew

Try adding some mozzarella cheese shreds! Makes 2 servings

Ingredients:

- 2 cups diced ham
- 1 can condensed cream of broccoli soup
- 4-6 cups of water
- 1 can low sodium garbanzo beans, washed and drained
- 1 cup chopped kale
- ½ teaspoon onion powder
- ½ teaspoon red pepper flakes

Directions:

Prepare crockpot

To cooking chamber, add diced ham, condensed soup, kale, onion powder, red pepper flakes, uncooked ramen; stir in water; cook on high 15-20 minutes

Air Fryer Chicken Sandwich and Basil-Ramen

Add more flavor, marinade the chicken in pickle juice for 2 hours! Makes 2 servings

Ingredients:

- 1 organic chicken breast
- 1/3 cup breadcrumbs
- 1/4cup all-purpose flour
- ½ teaspoon smoked paprika
- 1 hamburger bun
- Olive oil spray

Directions:

In a plastic baggie combine breadcrumbs, flour, paprika; place chicken breast inside and shake until breast is coated; lay breast in cooking chamber and coat with spray; cook 15 minutes at 360 degrees; flip, spray, cook 15 minutes; place on bun with any desired condiments

Thyme Ramen

Beans make an excellent addition! Makes 2 servings

Ingredients:

- 1 package ramen
- 1 cup chopped thyme
- 1 can whole kernel corn
- 2 tablespoons pine nuts
- 1 can cream of chicken condensed low sodium
- 3-4 cups of low sodium chicken broth or water

Directions:

In pot combine ramen, thyme, corn, pine nuts, condensed soup; stir in liquid; simmer 9-10 minutes

Apple- Chicken Sausage and Ramen

Turkey sausage works, too! Makes 2 servings

Ingredients:

- 1 package ramen
- 8 links of chicken sausage cut in half
- ½ teaspoon smoked paprika
- ½ celery salt
- 1 teaspoon diced parsley
- 5-6 cups water -or- low sodium chicken broth
- 1 package shredded mozzarella or Mexican blend cheese

Directions:

In a pot or a high-walled skillet add ramen, chicken sausage halves, paprika, salt, parsley; stir in broth; simmer 8-10 minutes

Spicy Shrimp Ramen

Also, great with basil! Makes 2 servings

Ingredients:

- ¾ tablespoon organic honey
- 1 teaspoon minced garlic
- 2/3 tablespoon butter
- 10-12 medium shrimp diced (cleaned, deveined, and de-tailed)
- 1 tsp Italian seasoning
- ½ onion diced
- 1 cup diced egg plant
- 1 can crushed tomatoes
- 1 teaspoon pepper
- 2 diced jalapenos
- 1 package ramen
- 5-6 cups low sodium beef broth

Directions:

In high-walled skillet over med-high heat sauté shrimp 30 seconds in honey, butter, garlic, onions, and jalapenos, Italian seasoning, onion, pepper in butter; add eggplant and ramen; whisk in broth; cover and turn down heat to low; let simmer 8-9 minutes

Crab & Ramen

Real or imitation crab works great in this recipe! Makes 2 servings

Ingredients:

- 1 cup crab meat
- 2 -3 scallions diced
- 2 cups diced bok choy
- ½ can low sodium potatoes diced
- 1 package ramen
- 1 tsp black pepper or red pepper flakes
- 1 tsp lemon peel or orange peel
- 1 bay leaf
- ½ cup low sodium crab juice
- 4-5 cups low sodium chicken, vegetable, or a seafood stock

Directions:

In high-walled skillet warmed over med-high heat, add crab meat, scallions, bok choy, potatoes, ramen, pepper or flakes, peel, bay leaf; stir in crab juice and stock; bring to boil, turn down heat, cover, simmer 8-9 minutes

Shrimp & Smoky Ramen

Salmon, clams, and calamari work in this recipe also!
Makes 2 servings

Ingredients:

- 5-6 large shrimp diced (cleaned, deveined, and detailed)
- 1/3 cup all-purpose flour
- ½ cup panko
- 1 teaspoon smoked paprika
- 1 diced shallot
- 3 crushed cloves garlic
- 1 head chopped broccoli
- 1 package ramen
- 4-6 cups low sodium red pepper and ginger broth
- 2 tsp liquid smoke

Directions:

In plastic bag add flour, panko, and smoked paprika; shake shrimp in bag until fully coated; warm pot over med-high heat; place inside: shallot, garlic cloves; sauté 2 1/2 – 3 minutes; add in broccoli, ramen, and broth; bring to boil, reduce heat, cover, simmer 8-9 minutes

Pimento and Ramen

Mixing butter and flour together is known as a roux! Makes 2 servings

Ingredients:

- 1 cup butter
- 1 cup all-purpose flour
- ½ lbs. ground beef browned and drained
- 1 can diced tomatoes
- 2 cups Napa cabbage or shredded lettuce leaves
- 2 8 oz. tubs pimento cheese
- 1 cup cheddar cheese
- Pepper to taste
- 1 package ramen
- 5-6 cups low sodium chicken broth
- 3-6 leaves of basil sliced (option)
- 1/3 cup diced parsley (organic)

Directions:

In Dutch oven combine butter and flour; stir until it turns a yellow- brown color; stir in ground beef, tomatoes, cabbage/lettuce, pimento cheese, cheddar cheese, pepper, ramen, broth; if desired top with parsley or sliced basil strips

Chipotle Chicken Ramen

For something extra add some black beans! Makes 2 servings

Ingredients:

- 1 diced onion
- 1 tablespoon minced garlic
- 1 cup diced leftover chicken
- 1 can chipotle peppers chopped
- 4 oz. tomato sauce
- 1 tsp celery salt
- 1 teaspoon Mexican seasoning (such as Tajin)
- 1 package ramen
- 4-6 cups low sodium chicken or beef broth

Directions:

In a high-walled skillet or pot warm over med-high skillet, sauté onion and garlic 2-3 minutes; add chicken, chipotle peppers, tomato sauce, celery salt, seasoning, ramen, broth; bring to a boil, reduce heat, cover, simmer 8-9 minutes

Coconut Shrimp & Ramen

Good any time of day! Makes 2 servings

Ingredients:

- 6-8 medium or large shrimp (washed, de-veined, de-tailed)
- 1 cup flaked coconut
- ½ onion julienned
- 1 teaspoon lemon peel
- 2-3 basil leaves sliced
- 1 can low sodium cannellini beans
- Pepper to taste
- 1 package ramen
- 4-6 cups low sodium chicken or vegetable broth

Directions:

In large freezer bag place shrimp and coconut, seal, and shake; in pot warmed over high heat sauté shallot for 2-3 minutes; add in: onion, basil, lemon zest, beans, ramen, broth; bring to a boil, reduce heat, cover, simmer 8-9 minutes

Prosciutto & Ramen

Remember, always use low sodium ingredients! Makes 2 servings

Ingredients:

- 2 pieces of prosciutto diced
- 1 medium onion diced
- 1 bell pepper cut into diced
- 1 cup kale
- 1 can low sodium condensed mushroom soup or condensed potato soup
- 1 package ramen cooked as directed w/o seasoning
- 2 cups water

Directions:

In high-walled skillet warmed over high heat, sauté the prosciutto, onions, peppers, sauté 1 minute; add kale, mushroom soup, and water; simmer 8-9 minutes

Ramen Aus Jus

Great with mashed potatoes! Makes 2 servings

Ingredients:

- 1 cup shredded roast beef
- ½ cup of shitake mushroom diced
- 1 diced onion
- 1 package ramen
- 1 /2 tsp Worchester sauce
- 1 can low sodium Aus jus broth
- 3 cups low sodium beef broth
- 1 dollop of sour cream for top (optional)
- Shredded or grated Swiss cheese for top

Directions:

In high-walled skillet warmed over med-high heat sauté onion 3 minutes; add beef, mushrooms, Worchester sauce, au jus broth, beef broth, sour cream; bring to a boil, reduce heat, cover, simmer 8-9 minutes

Bacon Cheeseburger Ramen

Our favorite Ramen recipe! Makes 2 servings

Ingredients:

- 1 diced onion
- 1 package shredded cheddar cheese
- 4 slices turkey bacon diced
- 24 oz. burger crumbles
- 1 package ramen
- 4 cups low sodium beef broth

Directions:

In high-walled skillet or pot warmed over high-heat; add onion and bacon, sauté 1 minutes; stir in cheese, burger crumbles, ramen, broth; bring to a boil, reduce heat, cover, simmer 8-9 minutes

Ramen, Bean and Bacon Soup

Best served with egg or spring rolls! Makes 2 servings

Ingredients:

- 1 package ramen
- 1 can low sodium garbanzo beans washed
- 1 diced onion
- 2 sliced carrots
- 3 slices of bacon diced
- 2 diced jalapenos
- 1 package shredded Monterey jack cheese
- 4-6 cups water or low sodium red pepper and ginger broth

Directions:

In a high-walled skillet warmed over med-high heat sauté onion, carrots, bacon, and jalapenos 45 seconds; add uncooked ramen, cheese, and broth; bring to a boil, reduce heat, cover, simmer 8-9 minutes

Bleu Ramen

Always opt for low sodium & organic ingredients! Makes 2 servings

Ingredients:

- 2/3 cup diced ham
- 1 cup shredded chicken
- 1/2 tsp black pepper
- 1 diced onion
- 1 diced stalk celery
- 1 teaspoon minced garlic
- 1 package ramen
- 4-5 cups low sodium chicken broth or water
- 1 cup shredded mozzarella and provolone
- 1 cup shredded cheddar cheese

Directions:

In high-walled skillet or pot warmed over med-high heat, sauté onion, celery, and garlic for 3 minutes; add in chicken, ham, pepper, ramen, broth; bring to a boil, reduce heat, cover, simmer 8-9 minutes; remove for heat, transfer to plate/bowl, top with cheese

Siracha Ranch Ramen

Also, great with chicken! Makes 2 servings

Ingredients:

- 1 cup diced shrimp (cleaned, de-veined)
- 1 Tbsp each: siracha
- ½ packet ranch seasoning
- 1 teaspoon cayenne pepper
- 1 can crushed tomatoes low sodium
- 2/3 cup whole kernel sweet corn
- 1 can black or kidney beans, washed and drained
- Diced parsley or oregano for topping
- 1/3 cup shredded cheddar cheese

Directions:

In large pot or high sided skillet, mix together shrimp, ranch seasoning, chili powder, lettuce, tomatoes, corn, black beans; pour in beef broth; bring to a boil, reduce, cover, simmer 8-9 minutes; remove, transfer to plate/bowl, top with cheese and herbs/spices

Pepperoni Pizza with Ramen

A great after school snack! Makes 2 servings

Ingredients:

- ½ Tbsp olive oil
- 1 ½ tsp minced garlic
- 1 package bite size turkey pepperoni
- 2 cups Italian sausage or turkey or chicken sausage
- 1/3 tsp Italian seasoning
- 1 can no-salt crushed tomatoes
- 4-6 cups low sodium beef broth
- 1 ½ cups shredded mozzarella cheese or pizza blend cheese

Directions:

In skillet cook sausage, drain, keep approx. 1 tsp of grease in skillet, put back in skillet and sauté onions and garlic in it for 2-3 minutes; add pepperoni, seasoning, tomatoes, broth; remove, transfer to bowl or plate and top with cheese

Chicken Sausage in a Red Pepper and Ginger Broth

Chicken sausage is another excellent source of low-fat protein Makes 2 servings

Ingredients:

- 4 link apple chicken sausage sliced
- ½ cup diced roasted red pepper
- 1 cup chicken sausage browned and drained
- ½ onion diced
- 1 chopped red pepper
- 3 basil leaves sliced or chopped pieces of sea weed
- 1 package ramen
- 4-6 cups low sodium red pepper and ginger broth
- 1 package shredded cheddar or Monterey jack cheese

Directions:

In skillet over med-high heat add onion and red peppers, sauté 30 seconds; add in apple-chicken sausage slices, chicken sausage, basil or seaweed, ramen, broth; bring to boil, reduce, cover, simmer 8-9 minutes; transfer to bowls or plates and top with cheese

Cucumber, Zucchini & Ramen Pasta

Great summertime treats! Makes 2 servings

Ingredients:

- 1 package ramen cooked as directed
- 2 tub Greek plain yogurt
- 8 oz. sour cream
- 4 cups spiralized cucumber
- 1 cup diced celery
- 4 cups spiralized zucchini
- 1 Tbsp. diced dill
- 4-5 cups water or low sodium chicken stock

Directions:

In bowl mix together broth/water yogurt, sour cream; in another bowl mix together ramen, cucumber, celery, zucchini, dill; combine the two bowls and stir well; best if served cold; keep stored in refrigerator in an air tight container; will keep 3-5 days

Spiraled Tuna Pasta

Try it with feta crumbles! Makes 2 servings

Ingredients:

- 1 ½ cups lemon mayonnaise
- 4 oz. low sodium/reduce fat sour cream
- 1 tsp pepper
- 1/2 tsp celery salt
- 1 can low sodium garbanzo beans or cannellini beans
- 1 can tuna, drained
- 4 cups cucumber spirals
- 4 cups zucchini spirals
- 1 package ramen cooked as directed
- 1 package shredded cheddar cheese

Directions:

In bowl mix together mayo, sour cream, pepper, celery salt; in another bowl combine beans, tuna, spiraled cucumber and zucchini, ramen; combine bowls and stir well; str in cheese

Chili Ramen

A new spin on a classic comfort dish! Makes 2 servings

Ingredients:

- 1 package ramen cooked as directed
- ½ lbs. cooked and drained ground beef
- 1 can diced tomatoes and green chilis
- 1 can drained red kidney beans
- ½ diced purple onion
- 1 tsp chili powder
- ½ tsp turmeric
- 2 cups low sodium beef broth or water

Directions:

In a bowl, mix together ramen, ground beef, kidney beans, tomatoes and chilies, onion, chili powder, turmeric; pour in broth, reduce heat, cover, simmer 8-9 minutes

Red Pepper & Jalapeno Ramen

Turn up the heat! Add jalapeno powder to the burger!
Makes 2 servings

Ingredients:

- 4-6 cups red pepper and ginger broth
- 1 tsp jalapeno powder
- 1 lbs. hamburger browned and drained
- 1 can low sodium refried beans
- 1 can diced tomatoes and green chili
- 1 package ramen

Directions:

In pot mix together jalapeno powder, hamburger, refried beans, tomatoes and chilis, ramen; layout tortillas; stir in broth; bring to boil, reduce heat, cover, simmer 8-9 minutes

Ramen Italiano

Great for fun family dinner's! Makes 2 burritos

Ingredients:

- 1 cup butter
- 1 cup all-purpose flour
- 1 can no salt added crushed tomatoes
- 1 cup diced eggplant
- 3-5 sliced basil leaves
- ½ cup diced Italian oregano
- 1/3 cup shredded parmesan cheese
- 1/2 cup shredded Italian blend cheese
- 1 package ramen
- 3-5 cups low sodium beef or vegetable broth

Directions:

In Dutch Oven combine butter and flour stirring until flour is toasted and a yellow-brownish in color; add: tomatoes, eggplant, basil, oregano, cheese, and ramen; stir in broth; bring to a boil, reduce heat, cover, let simmer 8-9 minutes

Greek & Ramen Pasta

Try adding some bell pepper! Makes 2 servings

Ingredients:

- 1 package ramen cooked as directed
- 2 diced avocados
- 1/2 cup diced black olives
- 1 cup diced prosciutto
- 1 package shredded cheddar cheese-OR- Monterey jack
- 1 tablespoon no salt onion & herb seasoning (i.e. Mrs. Dash)
- ½ cup extra virgin olive oil

Directions:

In a bowl mix together ramen, avocados, olives, prosciutto, paprika, cheese, seasoning, olive oil; serve chilled; keep stored in refrigerator in an air tight container

Tex-Mex Ramen

Always use low sodium ingredients! Makes 2 servings

Ingredients:

- 1 diced onion
- 2 cups sliced steak
- 1 cup diced avocado
- 1 red bell pepper diced
- 1 ½ cup salsa
- 1 package ramen
- 4-6 cup low sodium chicken broth
- Shredded Queso

Directions:

Into high-walled skillet or pot warmed over high heat add: onion, pepper, steak, avocado, salsa, ramen; stir in broth; bring to a boil, reduce heat, cover, simmer 8-9 minutes; remove and pour into bowls or spoon on plate and top with shredded cheese

Pulled Pork Burrito

Try pinto, lentils, or kidney beans instead of BBQ beans!
Makes 2 servings

Ingredients:

- 1 cup pulled pork
- 1 can low sodium pork and beans
- 1 cup diced sweet onion
- 1 teaspoon jalapeno seasoning -OR- red pepper flakes
- 1 package ramen cooked as directed
- 3 cups low sodium beef broth

Directions:

Prepare casserole dish and preheat oven to 350

Mix together pork, beans, onion, jalapeno seasoning, ramen, and broth; place in dish and cook 30 minutes

Red Pepper & Corn Pasta

Great for meatless Mondays! Makes 2 servings

Ingredients:

- 1 cup worth diced roasted red peppers
- 1 cup whole kernel corn
- 1 package ramen
- ½ cup extra virgin olive oil
- 1 package shredded mozzarella, tomato, and basil- OR-Monterey jack cheese

Directions:

In a bowl, mix together roasted red peppers, corn, ramen, oil, cheese; toss; served chilled; keep stored in air tight container in the refrigerator

Cajun Ramen

Also, great with mussels and clams! Makes 2 servings

Ingredients:

- 2 diced links of andouille sausage
- 1/2 cup sour cream
- 1 small can tomato sauce
- 1 Tbsp tomato paste
- 2 cups low sodium beef broth
- 1 Tbsp Cajun seasoning
- 1 Tbsp diced onions, peppers, and celery (trinity mix)
- 1 Tbsp. cilantro
- 1 package ramen
- 4-6 cups low sodium chicken or beef broth

Directions:

In Dutch oven mix together sausage, sour cream, tomato sauce, tomato paste, seasoning, trinity mix, cilantro, ramen; pour in broth; bring to boil, reduce heat, cover, simmer 8-9 minutes

Author's Afterthoughts

Thanks ever so much to each of my cherished readers for investing the time to read this book!

I know you could have picked from many other books but you chose this one. So a big thanks for downloading this book and reading all the way to the end.

If you enjoyed this book or received value from it, I'd like to ask you for a favor. Please take a few minutes to post an honest and heartfelt review on Amazon.com. Your support does make a difference and helps to benefit other people.

Thanks!

Daniel Humphreys

About the Author

Daniel Humphreys

Many people will ask me if I am German or Norman, and my answer is that I am 100% unique! Joking aside, I owe my cooking influence mainly to my mother who was British! I can certainly make a mean Sheppard's pie, but when it comes to preparing Bratwurst sausages and drinking beer with friends, I am also all in!

I am taking you on this culinary journey with me and hope you can appreciate my diversified background. In my 15 years career as a chef, I never had a dish returned to me by one of clients, so that should say something about me!

Actually, I will take that back. My worst critic is my four years old son, who refuses to taste anything that is green color. That shall pass, I am sure.

My hope is to help my children discover the joy of cooking and sharing their creations with their loved ones, like I did all my life. When you develop a passion for cooking and my suspicious is that you have one as well, it usually sticks for life. The best advice I can give anyone as a professional chef is invest. Invest your time, your heart in each meal you are creating. Invest also a little money in good cooking hardware and quality ingredients. But most of all enjoy every meal you prepare with YOUR friends and family!

Manufactured by Amazon.ca
Bolton, ON

36382012R00065